WOUNDED
Sheep

How to Heal CHURCH HURT

Wounded Sheep

How to Heal Church Hurt

Dr. Barbara L. Howard

Mill City Press, Inc.
2301 Lucien Way #415
Maitland, FL 32751
407.339.4217
www.millcitypress.net

© 2017 by Dr. Barbara L. Howard

Originally published© 2013 Dr. Barbara L. Howard.
All rights reserved.

All rights reserved solely by the author. The author guarantees all contents are original and do not infringe upon the legal rights of any other person or work. No part of this book may be reproduced in any form without the permission of the author. The views expressed in this book are not necessarily those of the publisher.

Unless otherwise indicated, Scripture quotations taken from the King James Version (KJV) – *public domain.*

Printed in the United States of America.

Any people depicted in stock imagery provided by Thinkstock are models, and such images are being used for illustrative purposes only.

Certain stock imagery ©Thinkstock.

ISBN-13: 9781545615188

Contents

Introduction ix

Wounded by Friendly Fire 1

Acknowledge the Pain 7

Purpose in the Pain 13

Glory To God 23

Balm in Gilead: Forgiveness, Love 27

About the Author 31

A Note from the Author 33

Introduction

I HAVE ALWAYS USED THE TERM "hospital" to define what we refer to as the church; the building of the fellowship of those who profess a belief in Christ as their Savior.

I refer to it as such because it is here where the masses of people come to be healed. They come to be healed because the church proudly professes that Christ is a healer. After all, He did heal the sick; give sight to the blind; raise the dead; and perform all manner of miracles related to healing.

I wonder why it was so important to Jesus that the body be healed? We may never know, but we do recall that he often associated the bodily healing with a spiritual healing. Just as He told the woman with the issue of blood, "Go thy way, thy faith has made the whole" (Matthew 9:22 paraphrased). Maybe Jesus recognized that when there is lack in the body, the spirit itself is deprived. So, the church is the hospital of choice for people who have heard of the good news of Christ. It is not that they don't believe in doctors or medicine, but they also believe in a healing of a Spiritual nature as well.

The people that come to this hospital are referred to as parishioners. They come from all walks of life, with all issues of life, with the desire to have life. Many come whole, many come broken, and some come needing to be restored. This book will look at the parishioner who has established a relationship with Christ, but for some reason has suffered injury either while pursuing that relationship or during the course of the relationship. These injuries are a result of the church being a congregation of imperfect people who do imperfect things, say imperfect words and cause harm to another imperfect being.

> Though there are many words to describe,
> How could they profess the God in our lives.
> He is such an awesome being.
>
> Though there are many words to beseech,
> The presence of His face can be reached.
> If you just let Him in.
> (poem written by Barbara Howard, 1/27/13)

If I were a doctor,
I'd write you a prescription.
Since I'm no physician,
I can only give the healing.
I can kiss away the sadness,
I can usher in the gladness.
I can pray away the sorrow,
I can preach about tomorrow.
I can sing away pretention,
I can teach about contention.
If I were a doctor,
I'd write you a prescription.
Since I'm no physician,
I can only give the healing.
The healing is the Spirit that lies in you.
(poem written by Barbara Howard on 4/4/13)

Wounded by Friendly Fire

Psalms 55:12-14
For it was not an enemy that reproached me; then I could have borne it: neither was it he that hated me that did magnify himself against me; then I would have hid myself from him: But it was thou, a man mine equal, my guide, and mine acquaintance. We took sweet counsel together, and walked unto the house of God in company.

"Friendly fire" is a military term used in reference to when one injures or kills one's own armed forces or allies. For this reference, being wounded by friendly fire is to be hurt by someone you know and care about. One would expect to be fired upon and maybe even wounded by the enemy, but never their friend. It does not matter how strong or how saved you are, being wounded by friendly fire will cause you to stumble. David was a giant-killer, but when facing the attack of his former mentor, he became a cowardly wimp hiding in caves. He was used to fighting giant enemies, but he never expected to have to fight Saul, his friend. In Psalm 55, he found himself facing even worse turmoil; he was facing his own son, Absalom, and his spiritual counselor, Ahithophel. Friendly fire can be detrimental to one's well being physically and emotionally, and most certainly to one's spirituality. One can only imagine the turmoil that David experienced.

We sometimes find ourselves in similar turmoil. We expect the unsaved to act in ways contrary to the Word of God but not the church. The church has always been viewed as a place of refuge and protection. The church is where we go to get away from all of the negative going on in the world. It is the one place that we expect to find peace and safety. We form intimate relationships in the church with the leadership and fellow members, often exposing our deepest secrets and feelings, leaving ourselves vulnerable to those we call our sisters, brothers, teachers, ministers, pastors, and priest. We are careful to gird ourselves with the whole armor of God (Eph. 6:11) as we go out into the world, but we neglect to suit-up for church on Sunday. Paul admonishes us to wear a belt of truth, a breastplate of righteousness, shoes of peace, a shield of faith, the helmet of salvation, the sword of the Spirit, and prayer (Eph. 6:14-18). David said he would have prepared himself for a battle with the enemy, but he was not prepared for this battle. These wounds came from someone he shared good times with and fellowshipped together in the house of God (Psalms 55:12-14). What we fail to realize is that church is not the place to dismantle our armor. Satan thrives upon our neglect to suit-up in the whole armor of God. In fact, we need to put on double layers of the armor when going to church. It is here that professed Christians muster the courage to be much harsher to each other than they would ever think to be to their co-workers at their places of employment, in their homes or even to their known enemies. It is in the church that hurting men, women, and children are preyed upon for sexual advances and favors, devastated by character assassination, mistreated by financial abuse, and most often assaulted with verbal abuse under the guise of a sermon or "word from the Lord". It is here that our fears are made manifest and our tears are made to seem out of place. It is in this place that the weary seek rest, but all too often find unrest.

Have you ever experienced a friendly fire wound? Have you ever been hurt by someone you loved? I would dare say that until you have experienced church hurt, you do not have a real sense of heartache. The pain from a friendly fire wound seems to be much worse than enemy fire…the wound seems to be much deeper, the scar last much longer, and the healing can only come from the Lord.

There is a fire whose flames are aloft,
A fire that feels much more than hot.
This is the fire of a friendship failed,
The fire of a hurt re-telled.
Not because of the hurt itself,
But because the truth gave way to death.
Truth is life and lies are not.
This fire is much more than hot.
There is a fire whose flames are aloft,
The fire that feels much more than hot.
This is the fire of friendship neglected.
The fire of a work rejected.
Not because the deed was not kind,
But because the friend was not of a kindly mind.
There is a fire much more than hot,
These flames are those that leave the spot.
You know how you can tell where the fire was,
The burn there is the darkest because,
The fire there stayed much longer,
The fire there burned much stronger.
This fire is the fire of a love invested, mistrusted,
    doubted or corrupted.
There is a fire that burns aloft,
This fire, my friend, is more than hot!
This fire, my friend, is more than hot!
(poem written by Barbara Howard on 3/27/13)

Acknowledge the Pain

Isaiah 42:3; Matthew 12:20
A bruised reed shall he not break, and smoking flax shall he not quench, till he send forth judgment unto victory.

IT IS OFTEN CONSIDERED TABOO IN the church to acknowledge that you are hurting, weak, or weary. Too often people are expected to mask their true feelings simply to demonstrate a façade of spirituality. People are expected to walk around like superheroes and pretend everything is okay. While we believe that through Christ everything will be okay, the truth of the matter is that pain is real. God tells us that in this life we will have troubles, but be of good cheer, there is an end to the trouble. However, while we are going through God reminds us that the feeble and oppressed he will not entirely condemn; for the broken-hearted he will not smother the flickering flame. He expects us to acknowledge that we hurt and that we need Him to help us with the hurt. David, a man after God's own heart, acknowledged his pain. He said "…oh, that I had wings like a dove! I would fly away, and be at rest" (Psalms 55:6). Physicians, with all of their medical splendor, are only capable of diagnosing pain after a patient acknowledges it. Once the pain is acknowledged either a cure or help to ease the pain, at the very least, is on its way. So it is with church hurt. Not only must you admit the pain, but you must reach deep and find the courage to tell the person that offended you that you were indeed offended. In Matthew 5:23, Jesus reminds us that if we have something against a brother or sister in Christ or they have something against us, we must go to that person (and there remember that thy brother hath ought against thee; Leave there thy gift before the altar, and go thy way). This may be a daunting task, but through prayer, God will not only give you the strength but the words to say. Christ reminds us in Matthew 17:21 that some demons can only be faced with fasting and prayer. Fast, pray and seek God's guidance for the time and manner to approach the situation. If you feel uncomfortable going to that person alone, you may need to take someone with you (Matthew 18: 15-16). Seek God about the choice of the person whom you will take with you. It should be someone that knows how to hold a matter and not found to be a busybody in other people's affairs. This person should also be one that is non-judgmental and possibly neutral of taking sides in the matter.

Furthermore, acknowledge that you need God. God delights in our need for Him. He desires us to call upon Him in time of need, out of our distresses. We have many examples of the work of God when His people called on Him. When David went out to face Goliath, he told him he came in the name of the Lord and he declared that the battle was not his but the Lord's. You know the rest of the story. David, a small, ruddy-faced lad defeated Goliath with a rock and a sling shot. All that was required of David was for him to admit that Goliath was too big for him to defeat and that he needed the Lord. There is a similar story in II Chronicles 20. Jehoshaphat found his city, Judah, under the attack of an army much larger than he could imagine, and to top it off the army was too close for him to come up with a plan of action. The only thing he could do was call for the entire city to fast and pray. In his prayer he acknowledged the power of God and his helplessness and once again the Lord answered. He told him he didn't have to fight that battle for it belonged to Him. The victory was given to Judah that very day. When we acknowledge our pain, it gives God a reason to show up and show out. He desires to be our hope and our song. He tells us He is a very present help in times of trouble. All we have to do is ask!

Oh what a joy it is to sing a song of His praise,
To tell the Lord of His goodness and Amazing Grace.
Oh what a joy it is to sing of the Hope the future brings.
A Hope in Jesus lets Freedom ring.

We sing a song to bring the tears,
We sing a song to calm the fears,
We sing a song to Calvary,
The place where Jesus Died for Me!
(poem written by Barbara Howard, 1/27/13)

Singing is for the down at heart.
It makes a rising in their heart.
It places a melody in their soul,
Where the half has never been told.
Singing is for the glad at heart.
It makes a breath within their heart.
It tells the story of a love unfold,
The story of a passion told.
Singing is for the melancholy.
It makes them want to be somebody.
It makes them have a dream come true.
It makes them have a vision true.
Singing is for me and you.
(poem written by Barbara Howard on 3/27/13)

Purpose in the Pain

Genesis 45; Genesis 50
But as for you, ye thought evil against me; but God meant it unto good, to bring to pass, as it is this day, to save much people alive.

AS MUCH AS WE DISLIKE THE trials that come in our lives, there is a purpose for the pain. It is often hard to see what that purpose may be while we are going through, but once it is over and we have the clarity to reflect, we see God's hand in the entire situation. To Joseph it seemed devastating that his own brothers would sell him into slavery. Not to mention being accused of attacking Potiphar's wife. But after the heartache and devastation, Joseph was able to see that what his brother's meant for bad was really for their good. He was now in a position to save their lives; a position he may never been in had it not been for the ill intent of his brothers and the wife of Potiphar. Yes, God uses these situations for our good. Romans 8:28 tells us that all things work together for the good of those who love the Lord and are the called according to His purpose. It is the hand of the Lord that brings about this good, even when others mean it for bad. Surely David thought his world had come to an end when his own son conspired against him, but wait, he says "… but I will trust in Thee" (Psalms 55:23). He was able to get beyond the pain through his trust in God.

Our trials are specific to us only in the exact nature of the event. The Bible speaks to us through the stories of old to help us even today through these very trials. Would you dare say that your church hurt was a storm in your life? Psalm 107: 23-43 tells the story of how to make it through the storms of life. The tempestuous storm and deadly dangers have brought those upon their knees that would never have bent in a calm. The scripture says "then they cry unto the Lord in their trouble". A storm has a way of teaching you how to cry out to the Lord. There is implication that maybe these seamen had been crying out to someone else. Maybe they had been crying to their loved ones or pastor, or maybe they were calling on Budha, Muhammed, or even Confucius. I came to tell you today there is no other name by which men must be saved other than the name of Jesus. For His name is above every name and at His name every knee shall bow that is in heaven and in earth and under the earth and every tongue shall confess that He is Lord (Philippians 2:10 paraphrased).

When you cry unto the Lord, there is divine reaction. Our savior is compelled to react because He told us that He would be with us always. He told us that He would never forsake us and if we ask in His name, it shall be done. What a Savior! Not only is He compelled to react, but He is commissioned to react. His very duty is to intercede on our behalf to the Father. We know not what we should or even could ask for, but because we have an intercessor who sits high and looks low, our every need is met. We have only one hope when dealing with our storm and that is the wisdom, faithfulness, and power of God.

Now, there are some lessons about character that a person can learn about one's self in a storm. In a storm one may find these 3 attributes:

1. <u>Courage</u>: In spiritual warfare God does not want to send cowards into battle. In the story of Gideon's army (Judges 6-8) when Israel was fighting the Midianites, the Lord told Gideon that his army was too large. If he allowed the army of that size to fight, the Israelites would have thought they won the battle for themselves. So, He had to reduce the size of the army. Initially they had 32,000 people but when God told the

cowards to turn and depart, there were only 300 men left to fight. In spiritual warfare, you can find out if you are one of those few good men.

2. <u>Commitment</u>: We are in a time when commitments are no longer taken seriously. Statistics show that divorce rates are declining but so is the rate for people entering into the sanctity of marriage. So, we may be seeing fewer divorces, but the numbers are only comparable to the number of marriages. The number of couples who live together before entering into marriage has increased tenfold since the 1960's. There are fewer people entering into marriage and the ones who marry are waiting about 5 years longer than they used to. All of this is because of a lack of commitment. Churches have experienced this same lack of commitment. The membership rolls have hundreds of names on them, but fewer than 30% are actually attending worship and even less at Bible study and Sunday school. David reminds us to commit thy way unto the Lord in Psalm 37:5.

3. <u>Contentment</u>: Contentment is accepting the will of God for our lives and being thankful for His divine providence. Paul said, "for I have learned in whatsoever state I am, therewith to be content. I know both how to be abased and how to abound" (Philippians 4:11-12). He is not talking about complacency. Contentment is not the same as complacency. We should not settle for anything less than what God has planned for us. "I know the thoughts I think toward

you, to prosper and not to harm you. To give you an expected end" (Jeremiah 29:11 paraphrased). We should not be complacent. God says no good thing will He withhold from us. And we must remember that the promises of God are yea and in Him Amen. At times Paul experienced definite financial and material need and at other times he experienced an overflow. He said he learned how to be content both in need and in plenty. It is often difficult, to say the least, to find purpose in the pain while we are going through, but if you will take time to reflect, pray and study the word of God, He will show you just what the purpose is. It could be a major character flaw that needs your attention or it could just be that God needed you to call on Him instead of handling things yourself. Whatever the purpose, there is one thing that holds true, God loves you and He cares.

Not only does God allow you to reflect on your own character, but it is also in times of storm that the character of those close to you can be evaluated.

1. Fair weather friend- These are the ones that will be nowhere to be found when you need them. They will talk a good game, but when the proverbial "all hell breaks loose", they leave you hanging high and dry. You can predict who those friends will be by the way they talk to you about others. If they are quick to carry you a bone about the situations of other people, they are indicating they will not be trusted when you need them. Anyone that

cannot be trusted is also by the very definition, untrustworthy. Untrustworthy is a character trait that we do not desire.

2. Here today and gone tomorrow friend- These are the ones that may answer the phone or they may not. They may be there when you need them, but they may not be there the next time you need them. This is not all bad because at least they can be there some of the time. Certain situations or circumstances may prevent them from being there as much as you want them to be, or even as much as they would want to be. These friends may be held on to, but just know that when you need them most, they may not be there. Their character flaw is a lack of commitment to the friendship.

3. Never knew you friend- this is the friend that was never fitting of the term at all. These are the ones that will deny knowing you at the drop of a dime. These "phonies", will see your number and let the phone ring. They will hear you calling them and walk on by. They will see you stranded and blow their horn as they pass on by. They will know you are hungry and won't feed you; see you naked and won't clothe you. These are the ones that the scripture declares "depart from me, you workers of iniquity. I never knew you" (Luke 13:27 paraphrased). These friends have no character at all. You definitely want to stay away from them.

It must be stated though that each of these "friends" have their purpose. If for no other reason, than so that you may be able to help someone else to identify them and save them some trouble. Yes, we are our brother's keeper. The trials that we go through should help someone else. Our testimony should make it easier for them, so they will not have to suffer the same things we did. "We then that are strong, must bear the infirmities of the weak" (Romans 15:1 paraphrased).

> Am I my brothers' keeper?
> The scriptures tell me so.
> Am I my brothers' keeper?
> The world would tell you "no".
> Am I my brothers' keeper?
> Yes, we are indeed.
> A brother created by God above, to help the one in need.
> (poem written by Barbara Howard, 1/27/13)

I can find no purpose,
In making people cry.
I can find no purpose,
I shall not tell a lie.
I know there is a reason.
There really has to be.
It's okay to ask the Lord, "Jesus, why me?!?"
I can find no purpose,
In pain and agony,
Especially since Jesus died and gave us victory.
I find no purpose in the pain,
I can not tell a lie.
I just wish it wasn't me that always had to cry.
I find no purpose in my pain.
No lesson to be learned.
Just a place inside of me that has to be returned.
Returned to the state that Jesus left it in,
Before the devil made his way,
Into the heart of a friend.
I can find no purpose,
There is no defeat.
Jesus won that battle,
When HE left Calvary.
(poem written by Barbara Howard on 4/4/13)

Glory To God

Psalm 124
If it had not been the LORD who was on our side, when men rose up against us.

It may seem odd to some, that during tribulation we should give praise. We often associate praise with celebrating a good thing. This may be so, but there is power in praise. One songwriter says, "praise confuses the enemy" (Praise Him In Advance, Marvin Sapp). When we give a compliment to the person on our job that has been giving us the most trouble, it causes them to hesitate and maybe even reevaluate themselves and why they are being a bother to us. They likely will become our friend. For God, praise reminds Him of the promise He gave us. He said if we praise His name, we would never be ashamed (Joel 2:26). Recall the story of Judah in 2 Chronicles 20:13-30. They sang praises to God, and the Lord set an ambush against their enemies. Their enemies were defeated and Judah was blessed with their spoils. Not only that, other potential enemies heard of the way the Lord had delivered them and they did not dare come against them.

Praise stirs up something in the heavenly realm. Many have heard it said, "when the praises go up, the blessings come down" (Author Unknown). Psalms 67: 5-7 establishes this very thing. "Let the people praise thee, O God; let all the people praise thee. Then shall the earth yield her increase; and God, even our own God, shall bless us. God shall bless us; and all the ends of the earth shall fear him". It is a good thing to praise the Lord.

> Praise the Lord with thine lips,
> Praise the Lord with thine hands,
> Praise the Lord in every circumstance.
> Praise the Lord with thine heart,
> Praise the Lord with thine soul,
> Praise the Lord whether thou be young or old.

> Praise the Lord with thine words,
> Praise the Lord with thine song,
> Praise the Lord whether things seem right or whether they seem wrong.
> (poem by Barbara Howard 1/24/13)

Really, we could never say enough about praise. David reminds us of our duty to praise when he said "seven times a day I do praise thee" (Psalms 119:164). But most importantly, the word of God tells us of our responsibility to praise, "Let everything that has breathe, praise ye the Lord!" (Psalms 150:6).

Balm in Gilead: Forgiveness, Love

Jeremiah 8: 22; I Peter 4:8
Is there no balm in Gilead; is there no physician there? Why then is not the health of the daughter of my people recovered? And above all things have fervent charity among yourselves: for charity shall cover the multitude of sins.

WHEN JEREMIAH ASKED THE QUESTION "Is there no balm in Gilead?" he was being facetious. But we know that for any healing to take place, we must make God our balm. Therefore we can answer Jeremiah's question and say, "Yes, there is a balm in Gilead". The balm is even closer than you may think. It lives inside of you. It grows inside of you. It manifests itself through you in various forms. It is the balm of forgiveness and love.

The Bible teaches us that a major step to healing is forgiveness. In Christ's model prayer He says, "Forgive us our trespasses as we forgive those who trespass against us" (Matthew 6:9-12). He goes on to instruct us that we must forgive in order to be forgiven (Matthew 6:14-15). As hard as this may be, we must forgive and there is no exception to the rule. Forgiveness comes in many forms. Some we may forgive by giving them the status of the prior relationship. Some we may forgive by letting go of the hurt and the person, and moving on in life. And others may be forgiven by prayer. Whatever the case, forgiveness must take place.

> Forgiveness is a word that takes many forms.
> And though it is desired it is definitely not the norm.
> The heart of a forgiver cannot be altered by a storm.
> The heart of a forgiver is not produced, but is born.
>
> Forgiveness holds the key to many things.
> Forgiveness is the value of a million diamond rings.
>
> Yes, forgiveness is a word that takes on many forms.
> When God made the forgiver, He made them many and one.
> (poem written by Barbara Howard 1/23/13)

Finally, there is Love. How does love play a part in the healing of church hurt? Well, if a church is rooted in love, then it will accept the past mistakes of others. It will correct the mistakes of itself, and it will allow the mistakes that are yet to come. See, we are an imperfect people, living in an imperfect world and we say imperfect words that may cause harm to imperfect people.

Be blessed.

The cross is where my Savior died,
But it's not where He died inside.
That happened long before,
When He prayed and couldn't pray any more.
The cross is where my Savior died,
But that's not where He died at first.
He died when the Father said NOTHING during
    His time of pain.
"My God, My God, why hast thou forsaken me?"
Was my Savior's famous plea.
He could have left us all alone,
But there was no one on the throne.
To tell the Father how it was,
To be a sinner, a saint, a slave,
To tell the Father of His days.
My Savior died upon the cross,
But if I left it there, we would all be lost.
I'm so glad My Savior lives,
So He can pray for all of us.
And tell the Father how it feels,
To live in sin like all of us.
(poem written by Barbara Howard on 3/27/13)

About the Author

DR. BARBARA L. HOWARD SERVES AS Associate Minister at Bethel M.B. Church in Lascassas, TN under the leadership of Pastor Freddie B. Carpenter Jr. There she has also served as a Sunday school and Bible Study teacher. She participates with the Mission Ministry, Social Action Committee and Lights for Christ Ministries among other things. After hearing and accepting her call from the Lord, Dr. Howard preached her first sermon on Dec. 10, 2006.

Dr. Howard desires to help those who have traditionally been oppressed through advocacy and education. One of her favorite quotes is "I have freed many slaves and could have free thousands more, if they only knew they were slaves." by Harriet Tubman. One of her favorite scriptures is I Cor. 9:19, "Though I am free from all men, I have made myself a servant unto all that I might win the more", and she tries to exhibit this call to service in her church, community, and career.

She serves in many community organizations and is a proud member of Zeta Phi Beta Sorority, Inc., where she has held regional, state, and local offices and served on a national committee.

Dr. Barbara L. Howard holds a Bachelor's degree in Biological Sciences and a Master's degree in Curriculum and Instruction from the University of Mississippi; a Specialist degree in Administration and Supervision from Middle Tennessee State University; and a Doctorate in Education Administration from Tennessee State University. She has also received theological training at Central Baptist Theological Seminary.

Dr. Barbara L. Howard has two wonderful children, Charity and A.J.

> I have the things God planned for me.
> He placed them in my destiny.
> I have the kind of love that sends things from above.
> I have the things God planned for me.
> He wrote them in my destiny.
> I have the kind of faith that makes things fall in place.
> I have the things God planned for me.
> He told me what they would be.
> I have the kind of heart that makes things fall into part.
> I have the things God planned for me.
> God wrote it in His destiny.
> He said, "You are my beloved daughter, in whom I am well pleased".
> (poem written by Barbara Howard on 1/22/13)

A Note from the Author

Psalm 126:5
They that sow in tears shall reap in joy.

WEEPING OR CRYING HAS BECOME A characterizing trait associated with women. It is often looked upon in a negative view, as some consider it a sign of weakness or being too emotional. It is also one of the things that most men don't do often enough. After all, one of the first scriptures we learn in our youth is that of John 11:35 which tell us that Jesus wept.

When I looked at Merriam-Webster's online definition of weeping, it said to pour forth tears from the eyes, or to express passion by shedding tears. The King James Version uses the words weep/weeping/wept some 164 times in the scriptures. So, this gives me the impression that the word is of some importance.

I am reminded of the passage in Luke 7:37-38, where there was a woman who was a sinner. The scripture doesn't tell us what her sin was so that we all may relate. We all have sinned and come short of the glory of God. This woman came weeping.

Most of the time when we shed tears, we do so out of emotion. However, I like the biological purpose of shedding tears. The biological purposes of tears are to wash away foreign objects in our eyes. Any obstacles or objects that stand in my eye, my tears to the Lord can wash them all away. That Is Good News. And for the sinner, the eyes that had once served as inlets and outlets of sin began to serve as fountains of praise. She showed a strong affection to the Lord Jesus. But it is important to note that this affection did not come first, and so it is with us. Our love is a response to God's love. We love Him, because He first loved us. And God wants us to know today that He hears us and He will honor us.

In other words, we weep because our God hears our cry and He honors us with compassion.

Let us look back in this same chapter of Luke 7:11-15. There is no mention of the woman weeping, but when the Lord saw her, He had compassion and He told her to weep not. He can hear our weeping even when others can't. Even when others fail to understand what is going on in our lives, God knows all and He sees all.

Do you remember how Hannah wept and travailed because her womb was barren and she knew her husband loved her most, but she could not bear him a son? The story states she went into the temple and she was weeping so that her mouth was moving, but there was no sound coming out and the priest thought she was drunk. And so it is here in this story. The Pharisees had no idea what this sinner was doing, when in all actuality, she was doing what Simon should have done when he invited Jesus into his home. It was customary to wash the feet of guest and anoint them before a meal and Jesus was no ordinary guest. So this woman did what the Pharisee should have done with the tears from her eyes. The tears, which were quite involuntary, poured down in a flood upon His naked feet as she bent down to kiss them.

When the woman had finished her worship service, Jesus said unto her "Thy sins are forgiven. Thy faith hath saved thee; go in peace" (Luke 7:48, 50). He had compassion on her. He has compassion on us.

David said, "They that sow in tears, shall reap in joy" (Psalm 126:5). In other words, troubles don't last always.

www.ingramcontent.com/pod-product-compliance
Lightning Source LLC
LaVergne TN
LVHW041551060526
838200LV00037B/1239